AF496586

# PENDULUM

## A Theoretical Framework for Change

# SHA VRILL
through
Hilary J. Allen

for

# Children of Light

Front Cover : Design  ShaVrill through Hilary Allen
            Artwork  Frey Micklethwaite
            Graphics David Knife

Back Cover :  David Knife
             Frey Micklethwaite


ISBN  0-646-26569-5   National Library Catalogue Australia





First  published on Internet / Zoist Bulletin Board / 1989
This edition published by *Dawnings.* Australia 1995.
With thanks to Sunflower Publishing.

Printing : Print Scene, Seaford, Vic. Australia
Printed on recycled paper


## Dawnings

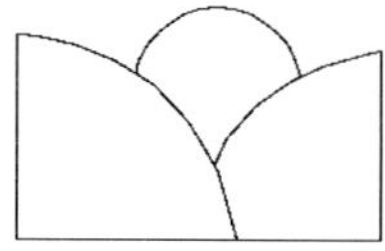

P.O. Box  1393
Frankston, Victoria,
Australia 3199

# Contents


Synopsis ......... ix
Acknowledgements ......... xi
Preface ......... xii

Chapter One — *Time* — Page 1

Chapter Two — *A Question of Values* — Page 5

Chapter Three — *Beyond the Pyramids* — Page 11

Chapter Four — *Ownership* — Page 17

Chapter Five — *Time to Reflect* — Page 25

Chapter Six — *The Keys* — Page 39

Chapter Seven — *Sojourn* — Page 45

# Synopsis

Pendulum has been chanelled. It is a theoretical framework for Change.

The group channelled refer to themselves as :

' Intergalactical Emissaries for the *Brotherhood of Light,* whose task it is to travel through our Universe, assisting in quantum leaps of evolution. '

We have come to know them as ' ShaVrill '.

During the last decade, ShaVrill have taught, debated, discussed, played and created  with groups and individuals. The outcome is invariably a heightened awareness and renewed sense of the soul's nature and purpose on Earth.

Through the book we have before us a guide, a thesis, a direction. The formula of $nf + 1 = c$ may be mathematical, yet is applied philosophically and practically to the transitional state of our Planet. and especially, to the adaptation of conscious souls dwelling  herein.

It is a thought provoking manuscript. It is recommended that it be read in small doses, pondered upon, and experimentally applied to daily life,

For the peoples of earth, it may be well-come.

Enjoy it, think about it, discuss it, play with it,
apply it....and if it works for you ....develop it further.


Hilary J.Allen
B.A. Dip.Ed Dip Y L
Cert. of Astrology

# Acknowledgements

"The creation and development of a project such as this has
involved many people, many souls and many hours.
We thank you all."

ShaVrill

*     *     *

The original was received, chapter by chapter, over the time period
1987/9. ShaVrill dictated telepathically as I recorded directly onto tape.

The process of transcribing, word processing and layout was
accomplished by Gillian Boatright, Kathy Foward, Jewlz & Les Bould,
and David Knife.

The artwork created from my clumsy descriptions has been brought to us
by Frey Micklethwaite and David Knife.

My personal thanks go to  Christy and David, to mum (Loree), to Keith,
Les.T., Denis, Ian, Jewlz & Les, Carol, Paul, Steven, Maurice, Jay, Patricia,
and the Joliies... and to Timmy and Jessie, my dedicated feline friends.
Special thanks to *All the Way from Earth* and *Raw Spirit* for your
music and inspiration.


So many of us have travelled our Paths with each other and with ShaVrill.
We thank and honour ShaVrill for their love, patience,
humour and wisdom.

Hilary

# Preface

There is so much happening in our world at this present time that we may be excused for vacillating between extremes.

Yet it is just at the point when the pendulum is swinging through the centre, that we are our most creative and potent.

Whilst we are in the midst of so much upheaval and disillusionment, we can literally grasp the creative force of the  universe at the very vortex of change.

We can look around us at the havoc and personal chaos  which is a consequence of this change, and lose sight of the very opportunity with which it provides us - a chance to evolve.

The growth of our planet rests with our ability to direct our attention to the synthesis of what we have, to embrace the full spectrum of what we are, and to overcome separative thought patterns with a vision of what we can become.

What we have is the opportunity to constructively, decisively and purposefully, direct our own evolution and destiny.

This is the heritage of many aeons of development of the human race.

Can we.....let's... play our part.


( the Little One )

# *Greetings*

# Chapter One

## *Time*

Time, is a guardian, our watchdog, hence we can understand why it is intimately connected with the gravity system of the planet. For that which holds us to our planet is that which also enables us to focus upon our time, our lives, our being upon this planet. If we move beyond our own gravity, our own aura, our own orbit, we may temporarily move into a timeless state, or of an even more complex nature, we find that we are into a *timeful* place. If we were to travel in space we would find that time within our own solar system would be a complex intertwining of all those times of various planets.

The relationship between the planets is of essential importance in determining time in interplanetary movement. Much of this will be found in the future. The challenge now is not so much that which we have yet to discover, but more so an understanding of what and where we are, at present.

What we are at present is as much influenced by what we would determine as the future, as it is by the past. If we were to travel into the future from this present moment of time, we would find people wishing that we had thought a particular way; wishing that we, their ancestors, had taken particular steps and had made decisions along particular paths.

Their thoughts from the future then rebound back on us into the present and influence the decisions that we make. So it is with our so called effect upon the past. If, for instance, we look upon what we did yesterday and how we thought yesterday (from our present stance in time), our ability to evaluate it, to analyse it, to learn from it, to accept or reject it, will actively effect what actually occurred.

It is extremely difficult for us to record exactly what occurred, for the very act of recording it, changes it. When we look back on that recording we so invariably recall so little of what it was really like. When we look at the past from the present moment we see in it *the causes that have brought about the current day effects*. We perceive it from the present and therefore change its very nature. This is of second nature to us all.

Time, then, is but a moment of consciousness. Time is a focus. Time is a means by which we organize and crystallize, the present. It is a means by which we are able to plan the future and measure the past. Time is a focus. It is imperative, then, that in the moments of change when so many of the landmarks by which we secure our consciousness are diffused, when so much goes out of focus and so much is blurred by changing perceptions, by fast moving comprehensions and emotions: - It is important that we have some kind of focus. Often that focus, then, is *time*.

The picture of an anxious father to be, pacing the halls of a maternity hospital, watching each hand go round on the clock; a focus; The waiting with a stop watch for a race to begin, when the entire system of one's being focuses for that moment when it will begin and we give our all; The moment in time when a baby takes its breath and it has begun. The moment of death, interestingly enough, is not as sharply in focus, and so should it be. Death is less clearly an ending as our first breath is a beginning.

Time then is our security, our stability, an anchor. It is an important anchor amidst any transition. On many occasions a New Year's Eve , a birthday, an important event proceeds, supposedly marking in time, something of significance. We build up a certain amount of tension and excitement waiting for that 'click' - the changing of time whereby somehow we are supposed to feel different, but so often  we do not and we are left with an empty unfulfilled anticlimax, a disillusioned feeling. It is not because the event is of any less significance. Rather it is because we have not comprehended the meaning of time. We have tried to hang our emotional and sentimental feelings on a framework which is purely convenient or instrumental. The aligning of that point, however, to a *natural* occurrence, adds another dimension whereby the full meaning within time & space becomes apparent.

It would be more appropriate then for those anniversary events or in the cycles and seasons of life, to look back on the past from the present; to look to the future and what we would plan and to use that focus in time for that purpose! For if time is used merely to recall the past into the present, then it leaves us with an empty feeling. Any point in time, therefore, must include past, present and future.

If we turn our attention also to plans for the future, on that anniversary event, we find ourselves far more appropriately using the patterns and rhythms of our universe.

The necessity to come to that point of zero, to intertwine and intermesh the past with the present and the future, to utilize the point of zero to plan for the future, to bring the hopes and dreams of the future back into the present, to bring the sentimental longings from the past into the present. How now, it is *Time!*

The Alpha and Omega. Aneos Drut. That which is, has been and shall be. To grasp that point of zero enables any of us, to move from one planetary system into the other without losing our sense of who and what we are. For if we can understand our movement through time we can also understand our movement through space.

If we can accept the point of zero whereby we are nothing other than an instrument for life's own creation, then we can move willingly from one space to another, without any sense of having to invade it. If we can accept that the time sequences we have known on our planet Earth are unique to our own gravitational system, we can let these go and move into a nothingness, willing to take on ourselves a new structure whereby we may refocus our consciousness. It is through the restructuring of our planetary time, to align accordingly with our true solar/lunar time, that we may find ourselves in *Real Time*.

# Chapter Two

## *Question of Values*

Let us begin with what is necessary, what is most important for all concerned. For that which is of common concern to all is therefore, the most important. A simple observation one would think and yet so easily overlooked in so many 'groupings' within this current era. The very survival of life forms is dependent upon fire, water, earth and air. These elements create the life force, the wellbeing, the comfort and the complete wholeness of the living life forms.

Let us commence then with these elements. One would think that the supply of those elements (fire, water, earth, air) would be of utmost importance or the first in any list of values and yet this is not what we find. The provision of food, for example, for any living form, is its first priority, the elements that it needs to survive must be there or it simply does not survive. It is not different then for the human species, proud as it has become, assuming that it is beyond such basic elements. It has ceased and continues to cease, providing these basic elements for its own survival.

If food then is of first importance in survival, would it not be seen to be that which is the most easily obtainable in any species? One of the guiding books of the planet, refers to a parable of seeds that fall on rocky ground and do not survive. Much seed then of the human species seems to be falling on rocky ground. There is less and less fertile ground being provided for the perpetuation of the species . One wonders then, why  the species is gradually becoming infertile, not only physically but also emotionally and psychologically.

Reluctant to perpetuate its own, hesitant about nurturing its own offspring, more inclined shall we say, to disperse the perpetuation of itself. Indeed, the human species is looking at its own demise. In its arrogance it does not realise that it can be so easily dispensed with in terms of the universal scheme of things. Yet the species as it exists serves a most important purpose. As the intermediary between many energies and understandings, beyond where it is now and the physical environment in which it finds itself; as the meeting point between heaven and the earth; the human species fills a *vital,* (in the true meaning of the word) role. Its perpetuation then is of interest to more than itself, for the Earth itself must depend on the human species for its own evolution as the "heavenly energies" seek to find their anchor within the whole.

In becoming conscious of itself then, the human species must face its own detriment. Its first value, albeit however primitive, must be *its own care, its own perpetuation.* [1]

Look then to the scale of priorities in all societies and we see that the four elements, - water, air, earth and fire - are costly.

The health of the species is important to all.

One finds instead that entertainment is much more easily attainable and less expensive in all senses of the word, than the very elements necessary to the survival of the species. A strange detour indeed ... However, it leads us to the second of values.

The human species, in its seeking of entertainment, in its seeking of extending itself beyond itself, albeit to the earth or heavens, weaves for itself a consciousness, a need and a value which once again is vital to its role within the universe; *that of the ability to take itself beyond where it is.* [2]

This can be seen in any given aspects of any society, in ritual, festivity, entertainment, creativity, education, intellect, technology .

. . . any aspect of human beings extending itself beyond where it is, is in fact a confirmation of its role. If, this is its second value in order of priority, the very creativity, the seeking, the exploring, the wondering and the delight - the 'original innocence' of the species, is of vital importance in its role. For were it not to reach beyond itself, it would not know there is a heaven let alone to reach it. And in its reaching for the heavens it stretches itself beyond where it is and becomes the 'rod which attracts the light'.

This visual image of attracting such condensed energy as lightning leads us to the third value, *"energy."* [3]

Energy at present is being seen as a means to provide for the first two values or needs: the survival of the species in heat, production of food, the collection and redistribution of water and the tilling of the earth. The purification of the air is one area into which the species will venture very rapidly. Energy is to be used for the survival first and *then* for the diversification of the human being beyond where it is. The use of energy can be seen in entertainment, in industry, in education, in movement (mobility), in wonderment, in science, in discovery . . . yet energy has a value of its own. Having been seen as a means to an end, we now move into a phase of discovering that energy has an existence of its own. In the past it has been seen as something to be generated, to be used, exploited, manipulated, developed and discovered.

It is on the final threshold of being discovered that we find ourselves moving into a different understanding.

The mental leap of that understanding takes us into the solar family.

Energy exists. Energy is!

Energy has a mind of its own.  It is spirited..  Energy takes on its own individual character as it diversifies through the universe.  Just as you will find sheet lightning and forked lightning seeking its earth, so you will find as many forms of energy in existence throughout your solar family.


It is the ability to understand that these energies exist, that they have their own characters, that they have their own destination, their own manners of moving, their own personalities ( that energies manifest, that they are there! ). This understanding then, is the means to open travel.  For it is not the ability to produce its own energy that will enable the human species to travel through space, rather it is the ability to understand the inter and *intra* energies that exist in all forms throughout the planet, albeit around individual planets, be it in the spaces between those planets, be it in the meeting of gridlines - the forces, the intertwinings of zillions of different energy forms across this universe of which we are a part.

Aah . . . .

The ability to "tune-in" to any one of these energies is the means by which free travel can be discovered, acquired, achieved, explored, and most of all enjoyed.  It is the freedom of knowing that one is not exploiting or using or abusing, but rather **riding what is.**  The difference then between a motorboat and a surfboard is a wonder upon which to ponder.

The fourth value . . .

The fourth value combines a number of different areas of the human race.

That which is beyond the planet Earth at this stage, intertwines a number of different aspects into one concept.  As such there is no word then,terminology, expression within the vocabulary.  Let us think about the rite of ponderance: life and death, change, metamorphosis, healing, goodwill,  the negative and positive energies.  We have here an area of the human being, often referred to as *growth*[4] i.e. movement from one phase to another.  The difficulty is that if one cannot visualise what one is moving to, one cannot see that it is movement.  Hence, death is seen as a doorway or gateway . . . as to what is beyond is left to the imagination.  One cannot move backwards in growth.  A man of fifty cannot return to being twenty in order to understand what he was at twenty.  He can only search through the cellular memory he has retained, adding to it his imagination and his understanding of the present, "a mode of being."  He cannot return to that state and tell the twenty year old what he will be at fifty, *unless he steps outside the three dimensional time/space matrix.*

How then can somebody move from death back to life and recall or record, what is ahead?  The only way that this can deliberately, be achieved is for one to have intimate working understanding of the very construction of cellular energy.

Let us consider our formula:  $nf + 1$.

If  a  Genetic Engineer, takes the natural forces that are involved in cellular activity, in the very instruction of the cell and adds one limit, one equivalent pattern, it will bring about change.  To participate in this process without destroying the original, but allowing it to in fact enhance itself through its own consciousness, grow and change in the freedom of its own intimate design, is to move towards understanding.

Change then is to be valued, for it is in many ways an intricate summary, an interweaving, an intermeshing and a sum total of the above . Here we have the four values, the four cornerstones, the cube upon which rests humanity. Without these four dimensions, humans are unfulfilled, incomplete.

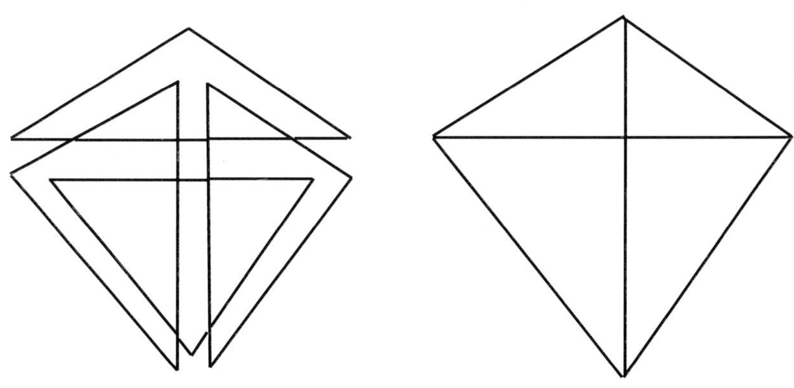

**Summary of Galactical values :**

1. The care and perpetuation of the species
2. The ability to create beyond what is
3. Energy
4. Growth

Chapter Three

# *Beyond the Pyramids*

Pyramids represent and in fact **are** man made structures i.e. they are not natural. They have been brought forth from the earth, shaped by human consciousness and *behold A New Creation !*

Now that the human consciousness can conceive of its world as a sphere, the imprinted perception of any structure designed to reach for the heavens must take upon itself a new dimension :

***That which is perceived as reaching UP must now also be seen as reaching OUT.***

The truth is expressed in the blending of both of these visions and yet we know them to be but a fragment of other perceptions as yet barely glimpsed.

Now when one sees the hierarchical structure as defined in the pyramids, it is natural to assume the highest point is supported by an increasingly broadening base extending in four directions.

It is easy to understand why, for many thousands of years, human consciousness has maintained an habitual manifestation and expression of the flat earth perception in its social realities.

The entire concept of slavery, classes and elitism must now decay, along with the stones of the pyramids.

*

Within the economic world, most human creation is expressed in the idea:

***Use Many To Make Much For a Few.***

It is the wastage inherent in the use of many to gain for a few, that ultimately becomes too expensive for the human race as a whole. The idea of wealth in its purest sense is the notion of freedom of time, energy, resources.  To be free is to produce the very best of life by living it.

In the world of ART, the love of beauty costs dearly. Land, nature, gardens, finery, beautiful creations, music . . . . . . are expensive.

Invariably artists (the creators) are impoverished and neglected in human social terms.  *Yet*  the love of that which they create is expressed through financial values, which ultimately reduces the lovers of art to a privileged few.

In the world of MEDIA, your communication systems, there are some who are paid handsomely.  There are many who receive very little.

The Pyramid structure can be easily recognised in social class, in politics, in business, in religion, in the distribution of food.  This structure maintains a few privileged, with the *increasing* base of the masses manipulated or ignored.  The root thought that flourishes as neglect and indifferent abuse of the physical existence, is this :

**'Being in the physical on earth, is at the bottom of a peceived universal Spiritual Hierarchy.'**

By allowing it to continue, you experience separation from the universe, feelings of resentment and bewildered victimisation, ultimately expressing rebellion against that which is perceived as oppressive, as above, as ahead.

In RELIGION you are witnessing a rebellion against  'The Father'  that " judged you unworthy of your natural freedom."

*Let us return to the sands of Egypt:*

Here we have the accrument of material goods to ensure the survival across time and space.  In the tombs of the great leaders of that time, wealth and beauty was treasured above all else.  How many lives did it cost to ensure one soul's safe journey beyond death?

The Pyramids were built by slaves.  They were guided and instructed to fulfil their part in an enormous team effort to build a lasting creation.  The Pyramids are a reminder for each and every soul involved in that project that they have succeeded.  The preservation of the very best of their culture and time has been successful.  This then reminds us and brings us to the new perspective achieved by sending a few (at great expense to the many) out into space to relay back the vision of your Planet.  By going ***up and therefore out*** into 'The Heavens', human consciousness  discovers a *non-hierarchical*  universe.

Within your Solar Village you have a pattern of inter-connecting energies.  Here the notion of inter-connective orbiting is a reality, not created by human consciousness.  *Now*  this pattern and perception is firmly encoded in the consciousness presiding upon your Planet. The social realities  (***nf*** )  which are an expression of human consciousness are *now*  in a process of adjustment.  This is a mutational process in totality, a realignment with an emerging perception of reality (***+1*** ).

If we superimpose the realities thus perceived one upon the other as the (***+1*** ) is integrated into the  (***nf***). A different world.

In the ***economic***  world, the concepts of shared ownership, participation and networking, pre-suppose a redistribution of profit gained by the many back to the many.

In the world of ***art***, accessibility is brought about by the reduction of huge payments to the few. Focus shifts to distribution, from *ex*clusivesness to *in*clusiveness.

In ***education***, centres are opening to all who want to learn, thereby eliminating the chronological hierarchy.  Education then becomes explorative, need/desire oriented and cellular  in concept.

In ***religion*** the mysteries are mysterious only to those not curious enough.  For any who seek, knowledge is made available: Insights and experiences shared are more likely to be closer to Universal Wisdom than that which is maintained as secretive and in isolation.

In ***political***  structures, the current pyramidical structure defies true representation and discourages the great pool of ideas, resources and talents inherent in the human race. Here you have a wondorous potential yet to be recognised: A cellular dynamic that nurtures ideas and growth.

*

The human being provides a catalystic role. The human is not separate from spirit or matter but is linked with both.

The Pyramids represent human attempt to rise from matter to the single point of spirit so preserving across time and space the gifts of human experience.

The top of the Pyramid is the closest point to *God*. If that is to be reality, the leaders of today in every hierarchial structure will be filtering down to the masses the accrued wisdom and understanding of the SPIRIT. If the highest point is out as well as up, then those at the peak will be those with the broadest vision.

Let us assume each human soul already has the Spirit Seed within it **now**. Then if the analogy is correct, you have all become Seeded with the light from the top to the bottom of the pyramid.

Therefore, it is no longer needed.

To move beyond the hierarchial is to embrace the universal perception of the human ability to reach out and be part of a wider and ever expanding Universe, so discovering the cellular like structure that enables both stability and change to interact in what is referred to as *LIFE*.

*A Living Universe that welcomes all life*
*as participation*
*in its own dynamic being.*

Chapter Four

# OWNERSHIP

The notion of ownership embraces the idea of **responsibility.**

If you own, you are responsible for . . . . . . .

Currently, upon this planet, the idea of ownership incorporates slavery of many for the benefit of a few.

' Let the People Go' !

*

In reality, nothing can be owned other than that which is truly your own . . . . . your self.

Even an idea is not your own once it has been shared, for the moment in time that you have the idea, is fleeting.  An idea incorporates the notion of responsibility.  An idea carries an impetus, an intention to share the idea, to manifest the idea, to create from that idea.  It by its very nature then, cannot be  owned for long.

What then is "Copyright" other than a civil request to honour the original idea ?

The very act of bringing an idea into form precludes a release into *Natural Forces*  which no one owns, $nf + 1 = C.$

An idea manifested becomes th *+1* which changes the **n**atural forces. The world is different for you having brought this idea into form. You are different. All is changed. The presence of the manifested idea takes its position in Time & Space. **IT IS.**

No one owns what IS.

The land you like to believe you own is changed by your presence. **You** are responsible for that change. **You** are the *+1* added to the *nf.* Your stay is temporary upon that land for it changes with and because of you. How then can you own something which lives of its own accord in harmony with you? . . . . . . always in harmony with you and you with it. For your presence is as real as the land itself. If the land becomes dis/eased in your presence, **you** are responsible for your being there and IT is responsible for it being there. **fini**

Nature heals itself. That is natural.

You heal yourself. That is natural.

You live in harmony.

To lease the land is the more realistic, yet the state of true being is all in harmonious co-existence. The notion of money for land is erroneous. It brings decay. Once land is bought, paid for, owned . . . . all that remains is the paying of rates for services to that land. This is a useful notion if services and the maintenance of those services, is costly. The **responsibility** for that land then becomes totally yours. The only reason why the initial process of buying land is still in use is the idea of freedom.

People want to feel and be free. Freedom means survival. Survival means being free to choose to survive. If one cannot afford to buy land with which one is then free to live in harmony, then one rents/leases from an owner whose responsibility it is to ensure . . . . . services. If the services are costly and do not meet your needs then you are limiting your freedom to survive.

The more expensive the land, the more the idea of having 'fulfilled' the responsibility in some way.  By choosing to live in harmony with the point in time & space, you create change.  That change is then 'valued' according to the social consciousness.  The social consciousness determines the amount of money one must pay for residency upon that land .  The more immersed you are in social consciousness, the more the land will cost.

In Truth, land is priceless, as is Life.

It is truer to  observe and evaluate land on the basis of the enhancement of harmonious living within its environ, rather than what is currently viewed as position / development / social accept-ability.  The real aim of the human soul is to maintain harmony and joy in its existence.

The natural state of the soul is as natural as nature itself.  How and with what does nature PAY for its presence, its dynamic existence, its being?  Be likewise.  Be fruitful, flower, give shade, *enhance* the world by your existence.

*

Ownership of people and things is another notion of responsibil-ity.  The owner of the objects, people, animals, plants . . . whatever . . . chooses to interact with those things.  This interaction changes what was.  You, the owner, become the (**+1** ) added to the Natural Forces.  A table exists.  It is bought and regarded as owned by a human.  It is then used.  Both the table and the human change in that interaction.  A vase of flowers added (**+1** ) to the natural forces of human and table changes everything including itself.  It becomes a point of being, a natural force in itself.  And so we go on, interacting, harmonising, changing, dynamic, being.  That process is neither begun nor ended by anyone.  That is no one's responsibility.  That is not owned by anybody. That Is.

Now, *the idea of ownership and responsibility emerges from the desire to interact and to maintain the control over that interaction..*

### *ie. The ability to respond*

Yet, the act of ownership changes all units involved in the interaction . . . so nothing is really controlled.

The only thing you can ever be responsible for is yourself.

If you consider  you are responsible for yourself and therefore maintain yourself, then you are surviving.  If you are surviving  you are free for you have chosen to survive and it has worked!

If you do not survive, the world changes for your disappearance (*-1* ) changes everything.  You have passed  over the responsibility to your soul.  It is free.  It is natural.  It IS.

Between you and your soul is an interaction, a dynamic harmonious cooperative relationship whereby you are both responding . . . responsive . . . responsible. That is ownership. To attempt to stop the other from surviving is to attempt to stop the interaction.  That is the choice.

An owner, then, is one who chooses to interact.

Money has nothing to do with ownership.  Money is merely the evaluation placed upon that interaction from the perspective of social consciousness.  Social consciousness changes as part of the natural interaction. So the values change . . . . . and it all gets very hectic! The interference in the survival of anything is a direct reflection of the assumption of ownership without the responsibility.

The freedom to choose to survive may well then preclude a decision to step beyond the social consciousness into soul consciousness and here we have the expansion of awareness harmonising with all that is natural.  For the soul is natural.

*In Time, perchance, social consciousness then emerges as group consciousness.*

*To see a World in a grain of sand,*

*And hold Heaven in a wild flower,*

*Hold infinity in the palm of your hand,*

*And Eternity in an hour.*

William Blake

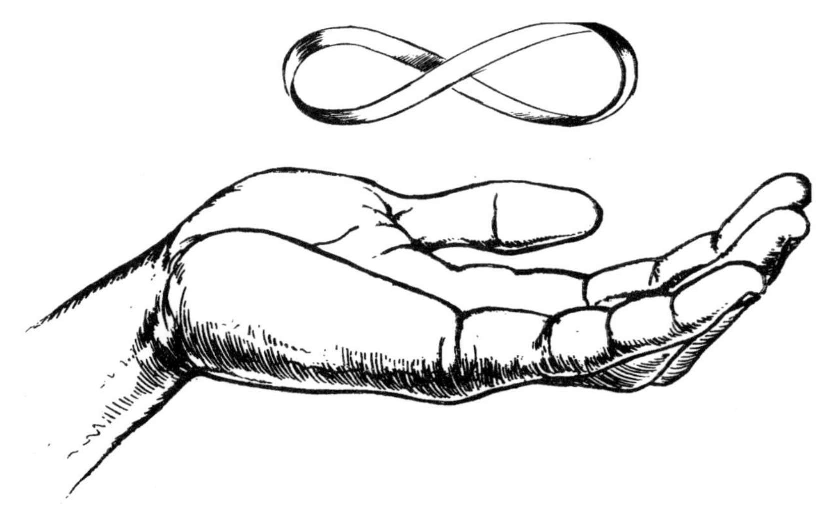

Chapter Five

# *Time to Reflect*

The point of zero is indeed the centre of being, the centre of one's self and  hence, the centre of the universe.  When we can remove ourselves from the polarities, the conflicts,  the artificial-however necessary - spectrum that has been produced over the previous era on the planet, when we can remove ourselves from this; cease to question things in terms of black and white, good and evil, heaven and hell - then we can remove ourselves enough to reach the point of the centre.  For it is at the centre that we find our true being.

The process of centering can be achieved simply and quickly. *Aligning* oneself symmetrically and relaxing the *breathing* is the physical beginning.

Then one need only ask oneself :

*Who* am ?  <u>Where</u> am I ?  **What** am I doing ?

This provides a Focus.

To focus Three Dimensionally, the question is of time/space. Fourth Dimensionally, the questions of orientation change as you do.

It is essential therefore that this human species produce within its structures, ***time to reflect;*** time being the focus, reflection bringing wholeness.

At present, the polarities that have been produced for us upon the planet have been askew. This polarity has in recent times been in the process of equalization. The masculine ray and the feminine ray have been adjusted to once again balance thep polarities that are necessary on this planet. The rebalancing of these two forces coincides and responds with the shifting and rebalancing of the magnetic poles.

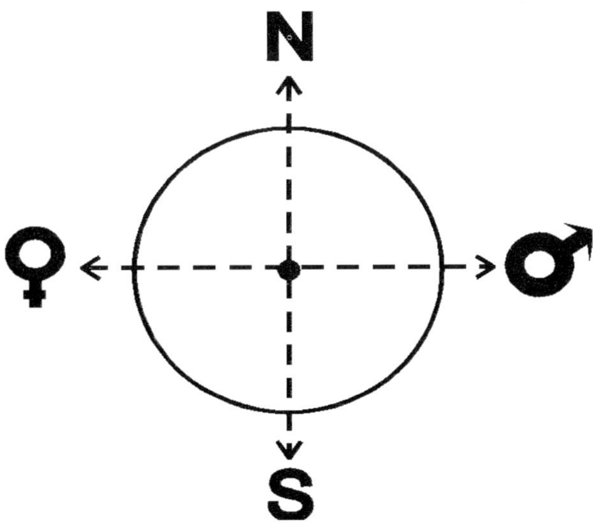


The energies move from the centre upwards, downwards, left and right. All are of equal strength and equal power, and if you like, equal importance. Ponder  on this. For here we have indeed the future stabilization of this planet.

Time to reflect then is time to come into the centre of one's being; to reduce one's self  from the vacillating between polarities whether they be between spirit and matter, between good and evil. Whether they be between friend and enemy. Whichever way you choose to see this, own it for yourself, for within us all for many, many lifetimes has this polarity been in effect.

It is essential therefore that the souls present now upon the earth realise that this polarity is shifting. The structure of society is most importantly the structure which reflects the polarities in the minds, hearts, souls and the very functioning of this planet. The vibrations that have been involved and have been the instrumental force in determining the matter of incarnation, the process of lifetimes and indeed the very world in which souls can grow. These have now changed and are in the process of restabilizing. The consequences for societies on the planet at this time can be devastating. Time to reflect must become then an essential part of all structures within and upon the globe.

The striving which has been an essential characteristic of the human race for what might seem a long time can now stabilize into a polarised, harmonious and most delightful equilibrium. Work, strive, grow, withdraw, isolate, retreat and then in the centre, find time to reflect. The very walking, thinking, time oriented, systemic schedule of the planet will begin to reflect this. Now, *activity and being* may emerge as the characteristics of your people.

The current generation of young people are well aware of this. Hence we have within our society what is known as the "dropping of the work ethic". Nay, moreso an *awareness* of the need to reconstruct one's time, to become flexible enough with one's time to be free to create when one is feeling creative; to be free to work hard when one has energy and drive; to be free to rest when one must according to one's own being and most importantly, time to reflect within, so that growth may occur from within and not merely in response to that which is without.

Many are there currently incarnated who have come to this realization. The system of retirement, relatively recently introduced, reflects this. Throughout the ages those of privileged classes and wealth and material comfort had for themselves, not only the luxury of freedom from hard work that "necessitated" their very survival but also the luxury of time, time to take holidays, time to reflect and most importantly, time to adjust one's hours and working patterns according to one's own rhythms. Resistance to this new change will only cause artificial polarities and tensions where there do not need to be any, creating *disease* on all levels of being. These polarities and tensions will release themselves, out of necessity, as the planet rebalances.

For those who criticise others who have designed a different pattern in their work, they will find within themselves in admittance of their need to stop. The balance can be there. There are more than enough people upon the planet to do the work that is necessary. The technology shall continue to free many so that this new pattern can be brought about for there is no coincidence in any progress. The results of that progress merely bring *change*. Sharing the work then becomes a balancing. Sharing the work, the play, the rest and the retreat... resting at the point of the centre. Take time to reflect, for when one removes one's self from the playground of life, goes within and reflects on what has been learnt, then one truly grows.

The reluctance to grow from within through this process has caused a great deal of stress, accidents, tensions, uneasiness, violence and illness. There is no longer any need for this. Time is the focus. By taking time to reflect then, the human being will find itself able to master itself from the centre within. The focusthen shifts from observation, involvement, absorption, experience, response: (a hectic process when is in contact with a dimension such as this )..... To remove one's self, to find the point of centre within is to allow the process of evolution to occur from within.

It is a significant point in the human race :


*Now is the Time in which this particular life form can progress of its own inner self.*

<u>The mastery of evolution is within the human race.</u>

*

The human race can then become It Self.  It no longer needs to be a pattern of response to impulse from without.  Nor any longer does there need to be an intervening force.  Whereas before, the development of the human species was dependent on external forces in order to progress and evolve, NOW  the evolution of the human being is dependent on its ability to remove itself from those external forces, to become independent of them and yet at one with them, and receive instead the *process of opening one's **self** to the cosmic forces.*

Hence the need for visitors from without, the need for divine intervention and the need for seeds to be sown from without, will **cease**.  One can manifest from within.  One can grow from within. One can evolve from  within.  The very genetic structure of the life form, known as the human being, can be mutated, changed, healed, from within.

What was known as miracles, one day will now become an awareness of the opening of the soul to itself.  And the soul in its turn opens itself to the cosmic forces, and then transmits (channels), guides, transforms those cosmic forces upon the planet.  This was indeed a secret of the Masters of the past.  Now, it becomes part of the  evolutionary structure of humankind.

Time to reflect then is the essence of the formula given

$$nf + 1.$$


The Natural Forces one can only understand when one removes one's self enough to reflect upon them.  For to reflect, is to shine back to it, the responses necessary for interaction.  Hence, harmony can be re-established with the natural forces.  The natural forces are there. They can be ignored. They can be abused. They can be exploited and they can be used.  They cannot of their own be manifested other than as a response to that which comes from *within* those who form the bridge between the cosmos and the earth itself, the human being.

What man *is* therefore reflects upon the environment in which he is, regardless of whether or not he does anything to it.  The essence of what he is from within brings about a response through the natural forces.  HuMan is the *+1*.  HuMankind itself is the *+1*.  It is responsible for change. The human species therefore is moving from a point of naivety.  It is coming of age and discovering that it is part of both the earth and the heaven and  that the bridge that it forms between the earth and the heaven is essential for this planet's survival.

The Rainbow species indeed.

In past times many species were able to reincarnate upon this planet: to remove themselves from their awareness of their true being and immerse themselves into the physical realm, disconnecting all consciousness . . . . . . . . . . . and the consequences were a devolution of souls.  A necessary process for those souls who wish to do so.

However the equilibrium, the restored and renewed equilibrium upon the earth, the polarities themselves and the balancing of these forces integrated into a harmonious centre will NOT be conducive for such devolutionary processes any more.  There is therefore a quite understandable and realistic fear and panic within those souls who have incarnated to devolve for they know instinctively, that their very process and purpose as souls here is complete and this in itself is a most profound lesson for such souls. The lesson common to all is the Universal Law of cause and effect. Souls do not die, they choose to disperse or evolve.

The clearing out of the planet therefore will be on all levels and time it is indeed to stop and reflect, not so much upon what has gone past, nor even upon that which must come in the future, but rather to reflect upon what one IS.  Many therefore will find themselves withdrawing increasingly.  It is most essential then that in this time of withdrawal that they find the harmonious point and centre within, and then respond from within  and allow this response to grow from within, out into the environment in which they find themselves .

Always moving from the centre though, will bring about quite a different response from the natural forces around, from fellow human beings to animals, from plants, from the air itself and most importantly, from the very core of the planet.

*

Time to reflect then is not merely a time to withdraw. Rather, time to reflect is a time to grow that one may emerge, regenerated, transformed and *integrated* with what it has learned. Humans are an adaptive species, enhanced by and with the living forces of immense diversity.

The system of education has promoted the idea of personal study for some time now.  Generations present upon earth  have experienced this. Those who have the privilege of having gone through this process need now to turn and use what they have learned and *apply it* in society.  For any knowledge gained which is not applied is not knowledge but  rattlings of intellectual toys.  An application of one's knowledge is the final proof of one's having learned it.  A manifestation and an integration of what one has learned, be it from experience or books, is the final proof to one's self of its validity.  Discard from yourselves then that which is no longer necessary.  Let it go. Release it cheerfully, peacefully and lovingly. Utilise and apply what you have learnt, be it from experience or information.  A society that does not apply its learning is **de**volving.  Now you have all you need to **e**volve.

That which has served its purpose well and has been  part of the society may have been useful but one must release that which is no longer useful when change is necessary,  The discarding of a favourite toy or a favourite piece of clothing or the releasing of a favourite pet into its much needed long term rest, so therefore many parts and aspects of  societies must be released.  The reluctance to release that which is past is an indication of the extent to which one is moved from the centre, for when  one is  at centre and has had time to reflect,  one is quite content to let go of all.

Time to reflect and ponder on the meaning of life cannot remain a privilege. It must become an integrated part of all human beings. One will cease then to condemn the art of 'daydreaming,' one will cease then to question somebody who is 'staring into space.' For as we now know, space is not empty.

One will cease then to question the validity of 'time out'.  For time out becomes 'time in'.  And time in, well used, reflects.  Time to reflect has been the privilege of the young and the elderly, the infirm, the wealthy, the flowers, the trees and  the natural species.

Our formula *nf + 1* can be applied.  It can be applied on a personal level and it can be applied on a most highly technical level.  However, it cannot be applied if one does not know or understand or have a responsive relationship with the natural forces.  All that is on this planet in its natural form has a purpose and that purpose is released according to the necessary (and at times unnecessary) calling forth from the human species.

We are most aware of what has been occurring.

We are also most aware of the calling forth from many who have begun to build a bridge to their  inner selves - the cry, the need for intervention.

However, should intervention become necessary, it could be far more devastating for the human species than the planet.  And those souls reluctant to accept the responsibility of evolution from within will find themselves responding with and to the natural forces according to how they feel.  That which is negative attracts negativity.  That which is positive attracts positivity.

It is most important then that those who wish to be free do not align themselves with external forces but rather, remove themselves, to transform from within and then to reach out and interact with the natural forces.  One cannot align one's self unless one is centred. Time to reflect, a focus upon which the human species will find Itself. The solar family is well aware of the need.  It is also aware of the evolutionary and spiritual changes upon this planet  and most importantly, the solar family is  ready to accept into its midst,  those who are of its own kind.  One needs to feel welcome when one enters

<u>*The magnetic polarities change*</u>

<u>*within each dimension*</u>

3D

4D

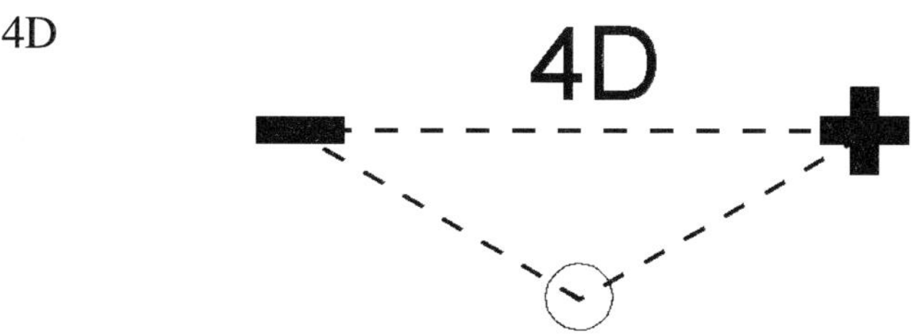


5D

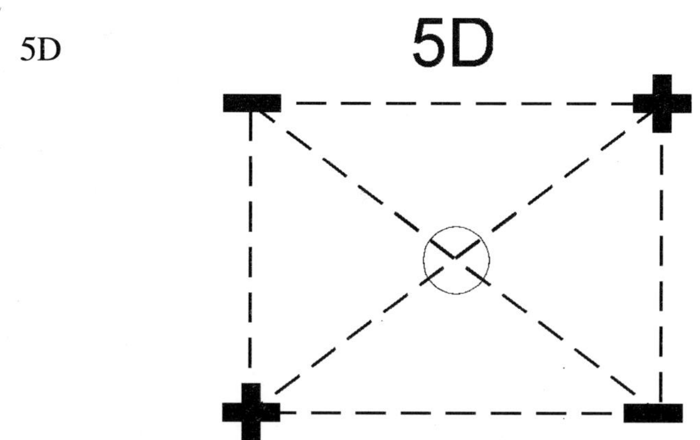

a family that is adversely different to one's self. To link ourselves with the solar family then, to feel welcome, means we must change.

Within, one will find all that one needs to know. The information needed comes from within. The inspiration needed comes from within. The knowledge needed comes from within and the attunement needed comes from within. This will no longer be the privilege of a few but is fast becoming the norm for the human species. Those who refuse to go within to find the answers and assume they are still there somewhere outside and all they have to do is find it . . . . . . . . they may only find themselves lost.

Teach your children to go within. Teach yourselves to go within. Whatever process you choose, the centre is the most important. For some, time to reflect is merely an ability to daydream and wander off into one's thoughts, for some there needs to be a structuring of meditative techniques. For some a need to be alone. For some a quietness, a serenity from within no matter where one is.

There are many forms and techniques and processes through which one may go within. Each will find its way. Allow each other then to find themselves. This needs to be the main thrust of all education. This needs to be the main thrust of all parenting. And this also needs to be the main healing process within the very planet itself. For when the outside of one's self is not in balance, it is the coming to the centre that restores the balance.

The vibrational changes upon the planet will be interesting. The speed of the planet (and hence the time ) will find itself changing and adjusting. The very seasons, the rhythm, the hum, will slowly change and adjust itself. The sound spectrum and light spectrum will restore themselves to a cosmic awareness and hence the physical mechanism itself will adjust. A most auspicious time. A most fascinating time. A most exciting, wonderful and all embracing experience for those who choose to be involved.

Amongst upheaval and change the point of centre becomes the anchor. The anchor widens and becomes the channel and the channel becomes the life force. Much there will be to wonder. Much there will be to explore. Much there will be to discover. Time to reflect will become most essential if one is to gain enough equilibrium to survive. And as each life-form itself holds its centre, so the planet's easing into its restored equilibrium will be so much easier. That which is above, so below.

The humans who walk upon the surface of the earth, affect the earth. If they are above, below reflects it. If heaven or the concept of heaven is above, albeit the solar family, the cosmos, the universe or other dimensions of understanding - if they are above to the human's below, all is intertwined. All is interrelated. All are connected. It is only therefore at the centre of one's understanding and being that one knows this, lives it, breathes it, becomes it and returns it back out to the world in which it finds itself.

If one is to travel into other dimensions, if one is to travel into other realms, if one is to travel into space itself and sojourn upon the planets . . . . . then the ability to be centred across time and space becomes evident. The need to know that centre point removes the danger of shock, removes the danger of being disharmoniously placed within other environments and removes the tendency to assume that what has been (and the very measurements by which one assumes reality) should continue. These cannot continue.

*Reality is being from the centre, wherever one is.*

Your mobility has taught you this. There are few upon the planet now who do not understand this and they will find themselves increasingly disharmonious with the changes on the planet and will find it, conducive to their own development, to withdraw and leave.

Those who stay and try to resist and find themselves clashing in disharmonious relationship with this restoration of balance . . . . . will find themselves the casualities,  will find themselves ill, will find themselves unable to cope with the destructive forces which emanate as a result of this restoration. To adapt or become extinct.

It is merely an energy vibration, however one's ability to cope with it is dependent upon one's willingness to go within and anchor within and allow changes to occur.

$$nf + 1 = c$$

## Natural Forces plus 1 (human) bring about Change.

Integrating the Change until it has become Natural, is achieved through the process of Time.

Whether this change is for good or ill depends upon the extent to which humankind itself, or the individual concerned, is still involved with the polarities. To move beyond the polarities into a Trinary Code is brought about by a natural urge to harmonise.

Take time to reflect therefore and one will find timelessness in which all is reflected.

Peace.

Chapter Six


# *The Keys*


What use are keys, other than, to open doors? What use are doors, other than, to be opened or shut?  The symbols therefore of moving over the threshold, of passing through doors, of needing keys, are all merely symbols.  In reality there is no door, there are no key holes and there are no keys needed.  Coming from the aeons of lifetime experiences such as that which has been, the symbols therefore of keys and doors have been appropriate for there has been a sense of being shut out.  Our perspective then, is to go beyond the need for the pillars.  To go beyond the need for differentiation into polarities , and, to use your own symbolic language, to ' lift the veil '.

The *keys* as discussed here and now,  are also *tools*.  They are the means by which the thread of life is extended, strengthened and enhanced.  This allows more freedom for both the soul and the manifestation of the soul in a current incarnation.  Therefore, whilst it seems as if one is moving closer to one's soul, in fact there is a greater freedom between the two.

The keys as they have been taught, have taken many shapes, many sizes, have been made of many different materials, according to that which has been needed in any given time.

A great number of your mctaphysical tools therefore, are keys. However, there are three (3) keys about which we would speak now. Three keys by which one may identify, release, invite, embrace and expand.

The first of these is the *Light*:

There are a number of religions currently upon the Planet that have referred to the *Light*. To all extents and purposes, the *Light* is that which comes from a Source   The Source of the *Light* is that from which the Spirit originally emerged. For the Soul then, the source of the *Light* is the Spirit. For the Spirit, the source of the *Light* is what you would refer to as GOD.

For the human being reaching therefore for the Soul, they reach for the *Light*. The *Light* manifests and expresses itself through the throat, the frontal lobe and the etheric connection point to the Spirit. The *Light* i s the means by which one sees clearly. The *Light* is the means by which one comes to understanding, enlightenment, comprehension, that "AAH!" of knowing. For this then means that the knowledge has been acquired, the tools are being used, and the process is in alignment then with the Soul, which is in alignment with the Spirit, which is in alignment with GOD. The *Light* then illuminates that which has been incomprehensible , misunderstood, not known. This can move extensively through the Universe. It brings about consciousness, it brings about conscious awareness, it brings to the mental body, the ability to monitor oneself.

The second of the keys is *Love:*

Traditionally the description of love within your world is relating almost entirely to the heart. For some, the heart (or the relationship of the heart to the will) and the desire / needs / wants, are incorporated in, the *Love*. In its purer state, *Love* is that which manifests indeed through that portion of the body referred to as the upper torso. The *Love* that passeth all understanding, is the *Love* which is aligned with the *Light*. For when the *Love* is aligned with the *Light* there need not be any understanding.

*Love* brings about an acceptance. *Love* brings about an openness. *Love* is the zero point of total *Being*, where there is no polarity, there is no negative and there is no positive.

*Love* is the natural force in the Universe. *Light* is the **+ 1** brought about to produce a *Change.* The resulting *Change* is the creative process and leads to the third key - the *Will.* These are not separate and yet each can be used separately and that is their beauty. Further, Love squares itself, for when /where Love flows it is joined by the Universal Love frequency. *Love squares itself.* When you love, Love loves through you as well as from you.

As a key then, Love is the means by which nature (nf) squares itself !

Then the process of All-That-Is, the process of individualization into that which can be used with more sharply defined focus, is again a known procedure .

It is LOVE which brings about the joy of individualization. It is LOVE which brings about the joy of returning to oneness, and this is a pulsating and dynamic relationship.

The *Will* - the third key, appears to be that which defines individualization. Yet it is not so much a defining of individualization as an <u>extending</u> that which has already been. It is the *Will* that moves the *Light* and the *Love* further and out into the realms of the Universe. It is the *Will* that carries it everywhere and brings it back. It is *Will* which touches the heart of another from which *Love* can then respond. For without *Will* one would not reach out.

In the total state of natural being there is no need to reach out. All IS that IS.

The urge for *Will* is therefore the third of the three.

When the *Will* is aligned to the *Love* , it brings harmlessness, creativity, progress, development, procreation, growth. When the

*Love* is aligned to the *Light,* it brings harmony, peace, understanding. When all three are aligned and connected, you have what is known as the

***Universal Life Force.***

If any of these three keys are apparently mislaid, or appear to be slightly disjointed, then that which is created, is only half created, it is incomplete and that is fine, for the *Will* may be withdrawn and the state of being incomplete , dissolves.


## The Mystery Schools

That which is hidden, that which has not been revealed; That which has been considered sacred, that which has been kept from you *. . . is the means by which one retains oneself in alignment. .*

It is means by which one can reach out, differentiate, individualize, share, grow, love, understand, and yet remain complete. Open the doors and Know.

*

The *Keys:* to *Love* is to allow no division. To know the *Light,* is to know that there is no division. And to *Will,* is to direct beyond any divisions that have been created.

The process of <u>separation</u> then, that has deemed that this knowledge, these *Keys* be separated, divided, hidden, sacred . . . . . This knowledge then, this process then, has been a process of <u>individualization</u>. It has been a process of *Will.* It has been a process which is now returning to itself through the heart. It has been a process whereby it defined itself according to the *Light,* or to the *Love,* or to the *Will,* but not all three.

The process then of separation, has been a process of growth, of experience, of coming to understanding, of embracing and extending oneself out.  The returning to the *Light* and to the *Love* and the *Will*, aligned, is a returning then to the knowledge and acceptance of LIFE.

These are the Keys of Heaven.
These are the Keys to one's true being.
These are the *Keys* to the *Door* that stands between oneself and what one senses is also one;s Self and yet separate.

The Door may be between the Will and the heart, the Love; it may be between the Love and the Light; it may be between the Light and the Will and so on.

This urge to resynthesize, this urge to reunite, this urge to become at one with one's Self, is the evolutionary stage, the true heritage, abd the joyful return of many whohave ventured out, and pioneered.... and who who now have many stories to tell !

The *Will* brings about Freedom.
The *Love* will grant the gift of joy and peace.
The *Light* is knowing consciously.

For many this is a new experience. For some it is a returning to that which is already inherent within their memory.

An imposition of Will upon another, is to invade their free-dom. Any suffocation or denial of in another is to deny the Love. Any witholding of knowledge or understanding then, is to deny the Light.

Perhaps then, the need for *Keys* is understandable. For by developing one's Keys, by developing one's tools, by finding and learning new skills, each Soul then takes into itself its own security, its own safety, its own assurance that : *it is Free to Love and to Know.*

DO IT !

Chapter Seven

# *SOJOURN*

Let us SOJOURN awhile, for a moment in time.  Let us capture that time, that moment, between the in-breath and the out-breath.  Let us capture for ourselves and remain constant within, at the point of zero, as the pendulum swings, from which this book was titled.  Let us then for a moment cease from the earthly activities.  From the mind that would distract and seek logic where there can be no logic, from the mind wherein the imagination may  expand beyond boundaries . . . . . . . . let us leave all behind and enter now through the Heart and the Soul.

Aaaaah!  Let us *Sojourn*  for a while then and sense and feel the world as it truly is, let us sense the rhythms of nature of which the human consciousness and human being is a part.  Let us sense the rhythms whereby one vibrates and acts and moves and behaves according to what one truly is.

To *Sojourn*  then is TO BE.

To *Sojourn* then, To Be, is to remind one's self that one is alive.  And in the midst of All that has been created and is in the act of being created, and is also the act of being dissolved, we will find the nothingness that has all potential and possibilities.

It is here that one senses the greatest potential of the human beings and the Planet upon which you now reside.  It is through here that one feels the lifting of the vibration of the *Light* and the *Love*  and the *Will.*

To *Sojourn* then, even for a moment before answering a question, will enable one to find the greatest and highest possibility and potential, to reach out beyond that which has been and draw back into the present NOW , the moment of possibility, that which can guide one to :

### Highest  GOOD  for ALL Concerned.

So at any point of decision, at any moment of pondering, at any spot of wondering, at any point of indecision or chaotic conflict, to draw one's self through the *Centre*, through the *Heart*,  through the *Soul*,  is to *Sojourn*.

As this becomes an accepted practice upon your world and within your world, the demand for instant response, instant decision, instant action, will reduce and dissolve eventually.  As one has mastered the pressures of time, one will recognise therefore, the pattern of time and how it is to be utilised within, as well as without.

The euclidian system of natural rhythm may then become a far greater rhythmic pulse of your daily lives and routine and the designs of your societies.  And as time-to-reflect is utilised within the training and  conditioning  and  shaping  of  young  lives,  so  it  will  also  be accepted naturally as part of the adult world.  And so we can proceed through the thought pattern we have developed in this, an opportunity to ponder.

The *Universal Laws* of which we have spoken are natural to your Souls and therefore easily understood from within and on the Higher mind levels.  Your task then, is to bring these into natural reality within the world that you are constructing.  This is your Heritage. This is your privilege.  This is your Purpose, and all those who currently seek for their purpose are ONE in their seeking and are ONE in their discovering that their purpose is *ONE AND THE SAME*, although manifested and expressed in its natural individual creativity, the Purpose is identical.

You are here upon this Planet, at this time, to assist in a QUANTUM LEAP of Evolution. You are here to carry the pendulum through the zero point and in so doing to discover the fourth dimension within one's self. For then it is no longer seen as a pendulum shifting but as a spirallic development of life in its natural BEING state, its natural energy, its natural pattern.

$nf + 1$, the equation is simplified, and given as intuitive knowing, that when change is all around you, you can enter through the zero point.

The equation marks for those who are ready, time of directing your own evolution, your own destiny in full conscious reality of the potential that is there and all around and within you, as human souls incarnate upon the planet Earth.

The Natural Forces are all that you have integrated and become within yourselves as part of the natural world with which you harmoniously vibrate. You are an adaptive mechanism. You change, integrate, adapt. You live.

A unit added to an nf that is not integrated, directs the process towards Chaos, rather than Creativity. However, you will notice that the symbolism remains the same. From whence does this *+ 1* emerge? From what great pool of the Universe does the *+ 1* of new knowledge, new insights,new awareness, new consciousness, new ideas, new theories, new discoveries, new technologies, new individual and unique human beings ? From whence does this come ?

This is derived from that which already **IS**: Worlds within worlds within worlds way beyond and within your own dimensions. Your Solar Village of which you are a part and are now invited to participate in as conscious beings of Light. The **+ *1*** is anything therefore that is introduced and added to the natural forces. <u>What</u> it equals, depends on the quality of that **+ *1***, (The strength of its Light and the extent to which the natural forces are in harmony). It can either equal Chaos, or Creativity.

$$nf + 1 = c$$

Either way, it is given as our gift, as a notion that through this you may become aware of your role in that Change, to move beyond any conscious urge to control. Expand widely enough to include within yourselves and your directions through this transition, all that is of the *Light* and to beckon by strengthening that *Light* in such multitudinous numbers, all those who are harkening to the *Light*, who within themselves, having been seeded with the *Light*, may then respond from that **inner** urge.

Your Planet is your work place. Your Home is the *Light.* You **move** through *Love* and *Will.* And just as you in your daily lives learn to interact between work and home, dissolving the separativeness which has brought about tension, strife, stress and unnatural patterns . . . . . so you can dissolve this separativeness and bring into interaction between yourself ( as you are in your home ) and yourself ( as you are in your work ), the extensions and expressions of the one self of *Light.*

It is through the *Love* that *Light* became and it is through the *Love* that you will return, once again to expand the *Light* of which you are.

As to whether you use this equation and the theorem given herein, (and the knowledge and insights that we have chosen to impart with you at this time) for the good of all humanity  infiniti . . . is in your hands.

There is no choice to be made, for the polarities are non existent within the centre, there is only that which calls from the centre, and that which is reduced or denied from the centre, that is all.

*Sojourn* then awhile within one's self. Find the centre point within one's self and at all times focus back within . There is nothing that can teach you this *except yourself and your own knowing.* By entering through the zero point, whereby you do not need to exist as individuals any longer, but hearken within yourselves to that which is unified within all . . . . .you come to know that your own individual addition adds and enhances that which already Is, and that your withdrawal of your individual consciousness reduces that which already Is.

## *Leave a Trail of Light*

*Sojourn* then - teach others to *Sojourn.*

Then you will find all the answers that you seek.

# Peace Be You